Pieces, Places, and Perceptions

A Poetic Journey
by
Kendall Belvedere Helmly

About the Author

Kendall B. Helmly was born and raised in a middle-income suburban setting. Dad was a university STEM professor. Mom was a housewife. One car and one dog growing up in a neighborhood with many children to share aspirations with. Later in life, the desire to write became an obsession. Starting as an amateur poet and graduating to fiction writing, Kendall expresses both the grit and passion of the human experience through storytelling.

"Words have power, good and bad. One's psyche is influenced by their interpretation. Through literature, we experience a silent world of idioms, and freedom of choice reveals our version of the truth."

Dedicated to my family. I cherish you every waking moment.

Contents

The Wedding Dress

I am worn and tattered, faded and frail, seeking solace on a store window mannequin.

I was beautiful once. Doted in lace and silk. My train once ran eight feet in length. The first wedding was a spectacular affair. Imported champagne, catered menu, and, oh, the flowers. Angela was a spectacular bride. Sadly, she died giving birth to twins on what would have been her fourth anniversary to Matthew.

I was cast aside and donated to a bizarre church. An elderly woman took pity on me, a dressmaker no less. Once again, I dawned a storefront window, hanging serenely in a quiet corner. I hung there a good long while. A blue feather duster was the only interruption to my silent routine. Then, by chance, a woman of means and taste came to my rescue. With a swipe of her gold card, I was off to the alteration department for a tuck and tat. My train was now ten feet long and fabulous, adorned with the finest lace. Her wedding was as perfect as I could have ever hoped for. Orchids adorned the room, framed in rows of roses, mums, pansies, daisies, and lilies.

The bridesmaids were all in a flutter as the ceremony began. Groom in his tail, father of the bride gleaming like a shooting star, both desperately trying not to expose their anxiety toward all the pomp and curiosity that was about to unfold. The bride. The bride was bursting with emotion, barely able to sashay down the aisle. Her thoughts wandering amidst the hope-filled fantasies of countless brides before her. She had not a clue to the bewildering question about befalling her veil.

Will you take this man to be your husband until the very infinitesimal of you has expired from your physical form on this earth? When she said, "I do," my buttons were bursting with joy and happiness. Well, in as much as an inanimate object could experience unconditional love. Oh my!

I am delusional with delight. The reception, the champagne, the dancing, and the fellowship were witnessed by all.

Alas, the eloquent fanfare must come to a sweet end. I will gladly accept my station as part of the bride's glorious wedding day memories as I am cleaned and carefully laid in a hermetically sealed container. I look upon my new resting place inside a restored steamer trunk, with all the other precious keepsakes in the attic. I know this is not the end, but a rest bit. It is a well-deserved vacation after such a wonderful wedding. I will enjoy the solitude blanketed in cedar.

At No Time

Tick tock,
Touch my hand.
Tick tock,
Race the sand.
Tick tock,
Shave my head.
Tick tock,
Slice the bread.
Tick tock,
Crack my bone.
Tick tock,
Seize my throne.
Tick tock,
Kiss the wind.
Tick tock,
Bury, my friend.

Baldy

```
h   c   t   f
a   o   h   i
i   m   r   n
r   b   o   g
    e   u   e
    d   g   r
        h   s
```

races

    to

      the

        floor

saves

  me

    on

      shampoo

Blacksmith Song

Accordion bellows damper while molten,
iron takes a molded frame.
The hammer strikes a hard anvil.
T-tang—T-tang . . . . . . .the steel cries out.

Thrust again into a glowing hearth while,
burnished slag passes to ozone.
Folding and turning with every blow,
T-tang—T-tang . . . . . . .the steel cries out.

Pound out the impurities and into the oil.
Dive into the pool and temper the blade.
Polish! Polish! Polish! Engrave!

Buy Now Pay Later

My dime lays on the ground, shining in the sun,
Next to my nickel, which isn't nearly as bright.
My quarter boasts a dull luster,
Lying in tandem with the others.
I put all my bills out too,
Trap the light in dark green hues.

Give me more credit,
No time for cash.
Just swipe and go until
The next fiscal bailout.
Will fill the potholes,
In my credit report.

Wall Street plays with diluted money.
Stacking lines of houses and hotels in the sand,
Buying and selling retirements, mortgages, jobs, and
food security.
As their toy soldiers advance on the new world,
Foraging mints to establish antiquated fortunes.
Debt is just a number,
Like stars in the sky.

Classical Iggy

My dog digs classical music.
I prefer Doo Wop to be precise.

When it's time for a little Beethoven,
I get a symphonic howl.
Big band or Swing will cause quite a commotion,
and induce glib restraint to my canine's delicate
emotion.

Bach and Brahms will get some plays turning to
evening shade,
As for nighttime's bedded slumber, Beethoven's 5th is
what he craves.
Rock-n-roll is more to my liking,
but Iggy will have none of that.
I had thoughts of a canine headphones,
surely the earpieces wouldn't fit.

It seems my constant conundrum will of itself not
wash,
suffice, my musical buffet will consist of classical nosh.

Crowned Crane

Please excuse my plumage;
I can't help looking pretty.
Shall I dance for you, no?
I shan't waste a beloved courtesy
on homo sapiens.

I would fly to a more suitable mate,
were it not for my altered wing.
Pinioned is the correct term for
my grounded state.

Sharing this cage with the Springbok,
what a hay burner, licking himself
constantly, and turds everywhere.

I fare better than the Reeve's Muntjac
and Asian Brown Tortoise,
residing closer to the ground.

Here comes that peacock.
No social graces, hideous to my liking.
After dinner, we played poker all night.
Except for the tortoise, he cheats!

Daddy's home

Mother's lullaby drowns my silent, blissful sleep,
Ending my stubborn tantrums touted by adolescent
wine.
Trumpets haunt visions of roller coaster menageries
beyond rem.
The dog sloths on a tender bone escaping mommy's
oven,
Reticent under the table for a misspent morsel.
Clanging pistons so familiar mediate the unopened
door.
HIDE, HIDE, DADDY'S HOME!
No wood to escape and camouflage my secret ambush.
Keys dangling off the knob, vent a creaked hinge.
HIDE, HIDE, DADDY'S HOME!
Ice stirs the tea pitcher. My nostrils fill with mac-n-
cheese and bacon.
Father says, "I'm home," as he sashays
down the hall.
HIDE, HIDE, DADDY'S HOME
Now the music stops as the invoice comes due,
ladings paid for the morning's outburst.
Father quells my anxious tears.
A loving embrace quiets any previous misgivings.
Plates are passed; bread is broken.

Falling Leaf

Brown and withered, I represent,
what has transpired in this locale.
Merciful to a wayward gust,
no attachment to the host branch.

Lofting over patchwork fields,
opportune to ride a nice tailwind.

Scorn!

Laying tempest in a coniferous cone,
soft ground may not represent the journey's end.

Squirrels jostling about expedite
my demand for fretted freedom,
straight down in the tumultuous ground

Too Much Pink

A hot pink nightmare,
Cascading up and down.
Broadway and Vine,
Twirling all around In frolicking fancies.

The pink hue in all its,
Pinkness drowning.
The other senses in all,
It's the perversion of primary colors.

Promenading in reels,
Strolling down the aisle
Parades of pink sashay
Past an ogling crowd
Consumed by a pink aviary Pink Infatuation

Wake up to pink eyelids slamming,
Down like rouged neon window shades.

Chess boards are checkered pink and puce.
Fuchsia playing pieces,
Passing along pink squares,
Moved around by pink diamond studded
Pinkies.

A boiled pink skirmish,
Twitter-piddled in pink-dom.
Pink hues in all their pinkness,
Perverting primary colors.

Parades of pink sashay past,
Googled glances,
Poking at my senses,
Choking on pink ozone.

Facing cheeks painted in pink
Perfection.

Too Much Pink!

Frail Mother Earth

Withered from the one and only star, ambivalent to its potential fusion. We haggle over dirt, a compromised tradeoff to this planet's illness. A puce garden of shiny bobbles and faster machines.

Race the toxic wind and bow to a checkered particulate parade. Vail the hero in his misogyny. Totalitarian desire presses a finite resource past a firm bipartisan voice.

Tomorrow will give legions the sanctity for phallic silos. Sloth assumes no remorse as fields of cornsilk yeomen sing work songs.

Commodity traders violate the senses, catching lilac and honeysuckle fragrances. We are drowned to the jagged edge of less educated profiteers. For a piece of silver, ocean foam will eradicate another berg.

Give Me Morphine

I'm old and past my prime,
For my legacy, there is no time.

My children surround me for a final glance,
As they ponder my last moment in fickle chance.

I have no dowry, no riches to probate,
Breathless slumber will prime my fate.

Slowly dripped into a withered hand,
Clenching the last grain of sand,
The morphine I feel, is working grand

My Goldfish with Coral Eyes

My goldfish with coral eyes never blinks at night,
too many predators lurking in the shadows.
Even in the wrath of ugliness nature stays in balance.
The coral eyes never rest, for they are hunter as well as prey,
hardened to survive and swim in the wake of larger game.

It is the way of things ceding to a bigger fish.
Avoid the hook and line, or end up a bounty on the Captain's table.
Nets will snare the careless creatures out for leisure swims.
The eyes are always scanning from surface to ocean floor,
anxious to feed and flee the reef marauders.

Working in parallel to snare a much-anticipated meal,
helpless if not for the sanctity of the coral reef.
Shelter and bounty for all to reap and few to exploit;
the reef has eyes in every crevice, lying in wait, giving
solace to another guarded night's sleep.

Them Grit's Never Boil

Mama's grits never boil, cause she keeps addin' water
Watches them like a red-tail hawk; she does.
Mama don't like no lumps in her grits.
They got to be just right every time,
That old stove ain't failed her recipe yet.

Auntie goes for seconds like everybody else,
People brag on her fricassee something fierce.
Well, her chicken's good, but it ain't all that,
And the dumplings taste like hard tac.

"Mama, them is some mighty fine grits," I say.
Heating next to the collard greens and catfish
Grampa would be right proud had he be here now,
Give us grace, and pass the buttermilk,
Ma puts love in them grits. That's the secret.

Hog Hunt

Dogs chase hogs through menacing bogs.
The hogs elude the dogs by running
under logs. The hunter jogs over the logs
in his clogs. The bogs sag his clogs so he
can no longer trot after the dogs, who
have given up chasing after the hogs.
Much later, the dogs find the hunter sleeping
under a log, dreaming of a grog.

Inheritance

Legacy allows passage across bridges of humanity. Prosperity quills the sacrifice of others. They are more qualified, but I alone will inherit the planet.

Do not judge; be justified in the quest for booty and lace. Mine now and yours of late will manifest my place.

Pen folds to paper. We are engaged in writing paragraphs, which will drown ignorance in ocean ink.

Wading in riches, my comrade lays envious of a lack of spoils. I wish no grief upon any mortal. Please allow for my shallow attempt at grace.

Pushing Boundaries

Standing on an airport runway
thrill-seeking under the 747's
shadow as it lands feet from
my locale.

No photo can capture the terror
of staring up the airplane's belly
as it passes overhead.

I am the ant they spy from a double
paned window. Destined to be grounded
for the duration.

Lady Carbine

Cold ground is my death.
My steel will oxidize to nothing,
having to endure a millennium of morning dew.

I avoid that fate now,
thanks to this red-haired blue belly.
Well, my relationships never last.

The previous beau to carry me
was straight shootin' Johnny Reb
from Macon. The best marksman
in his unit by a long yard. I watched him
bust the wings off a fly at 100 yards.
Unfortunate, for the union corporal,
the fly was laid on.
That was Chancellorsville.

I always held a special place in his
heart. The way he constantly doted
how I pulled his unmolested gorgeous
body out of the fire a time or two.
Cleaning me, shining my inspection plate
to a fervent gloss.
I occupied his days but,
Pauline, she filled his nights.

That little Georgia peach tenderized
many a cold darkness for him.
Made the best biscuits and apple butter

in Bibb County, two blue ribbons
prove it. Ray loved Pauline and
attested that fact in every letter
he sent.

It grieved me so to watch him fall on
the railed fence at the end of Pickett's
ill-fated charge. Were my barrel full
of tears, I surely would have rusted solid
by evening shade. So many boys marched up
that hill caught in a hellacious crossfire;
passing the test of manhood in bespattered
blood by ranks before them.

I would still lay resting against that infamous
fence post counting crocodile tears, were it not
for a red-headed Maggie's drawers
taking a liking to me.

So much so that he discarded forthwith that
three-band Springfield rifle he was dragging
along, I being the exceedingly more
accurate of the two. But, not in my new
companion's sights, I'm afraid; with four eyes
and six thumbs couldn't shoot a barn standing
inside, the bullet destined to find an open
doorway. Marvelous hand-to-hand skills, though.
He certainly knew which end of the bayonet
to tickle Johnny's ribs with.

Terrible way to die, taking a pointy dull
blade to the entrails as the reflux burns

unmercifully. Agony until the shock comes.
Then, coldness for a time as the lifeblood runs out.

The first soldier I was issued to after being
Uncrated and inventoried, it was not much to
my liking nor to anyone else in his proximity.
A boozing man and a tobacco chewer.
Ghastly habits, both of them.

Bathing was an option he addressed very
infrequently while maintaining the rank
of sergeant in the Union Army. I did manage
to stay in good working order. About the only
thing he ever cleaned, certainly not that beard
of his, with a constant look of cobwebs and
the smell of lingering leftovers. I guess that's
why they made him a mess, Sgt. The other men
did seem to like his cooking. He used me many
a time to hunt down large game. Those cows he
used to shoot out of the barnyards certainly
represented very elusive prey. Somewhat ironic
that my fair-haired rebel would end up taking me
right off the back of the mess wagon at the end of
First Bull Run.

A headshot is the best, though, whether shooting an
animal or
a soldier.
58 caliber bullet penetrates the skull, all
in an instant, the body falls, and the soul rises.
Still, a reverberated mess, though.

Weapons are cherished for their efficiency in
combat but I fit no bill when the dead
are put away by day's end. I must be carefully
aimed and fired to cause the needless death
of men facing the business end of my barrel;
solaced only by the hope of ending the degradation
of lost souls.

My Aphrodite

A foot applied to the brakes, and
travel is halted until she,
the object of my unassuming gander,
Occupies a seat.

Young and radiant in her beauty mask,
to rival Venus. Eyes that turn lovers to stone.
Frozen sterile, stealing virility from any man
subject to a peripheral gaze within
her idolatrous glance.

Rising from her adjacent position, she
pulled the wire, announcing her intention to exit
our bus through bypass doors.

Would she walk by, and I pass her goosebumps;
pulsating my stone stature. Compelling me back to
stoic breaths of consciousness, dream Aphrodite.

Night Swamp

Winding narrows through the oak hammock.
Jettison an estuary of plaid silt marsh,
Recline in the Geechie swamp,
Counting cicada skins on the porch.

Light ebbs to a bullfrog grunt,
Gator cruise the water's edge for a lapping tongue.
Splash and snap and death roll under submerged root,
Black water tenderizes a feast.

Warm wilted winds brush palmettoes,
Moon glitters catfish whiskers.
Sultry sheets of silent sweat still my stagnant, sheltered
sleep.

Ocelot

I was born in Orlando, I've been told.
My days are filled with planning my next meal.
Ask if I know jungles. I think not.

This makeshift canary island paradise
is nothing but shade, which I take full advantage of.
Dinner is promptly at 4 pm., table for one.

Just once, I'd like to take a shot at the squirrel,
monkey in the adjacent pen.
I am constantly taunted by rodents scampering.

About between bamboo shoots.
Time for my afternoon walk, 137 laps,
Equals one mile, breaking up the day.

I wish they would let the visitors gather,
near the cage, giving them a chance at a fresh finger
Or two. Lovely hors d'oeuvres.

Ocean's Kiss

The ocean reverberates as I pour sand from a
nautilus shell while rocks separate the ocean spray.
We Stand among the falling tide amid clumps of
eelgrass
as I wash the silt from your hands.

Prepare a bounty of seaweed salad for a picnic along the
road. Devoured in twilight under moonshine.
Together, we elope into a midnight swim.

Pining for a kiss, I can't hide
my anticipation of moist, salty air.

Semesters End

No more chalk dust on my fingers,
No slate, long and black.
No percolating screeches between syllables,
Or broken nubs on the rack.

Blinding highways cripple my mind,
Gloves hide my fingerprints in the sand.
We swing into the middle of an empty stadium.
Waiting for the zealous crowd to enter,
Shy to the center, watching.
Hoards gasp and regale at the dominant,
Feats that lay before us.
None to march the field in stoic grace,
Dancing on the water to the bright moonlight.

Stolen conversation makes for envied words,
As if the moon could be ransomed in jest.
Mastering the subtle art of a skillful eavesdrop,
Gathering grocery carts of reserve speak.
Malign the unknowing victim's verbal heist,
Unwanted secrets spill into a naive ear.
This thievery burdens my conscience,
I close my eyes and pray forgiveness.
Consoled in a neighborhood speakeasy,
Wine and song cater to my presumed silence.

Peppermint Rapture

A peppermint threshold delinquents warm breach,
ways with interior scale. The supple variations of a
cloud-filled sky.
Zephyr, will no more end a ravenous
appetite to voyeur pastel doorways.

The path remains wide open. No tumult in being a
proud
the passageway to seedling remorse, just a gaze of
particulates
resting among icons.

My outreached palm gives little praise to a parson's
rift, delegated in a habit of ministerial perfection.
Words
tourniquet sequential penance to a sweet, undercoated
treat.

Public Bench

Come rest, my tired pedestrian.
Sit and nature now will feed a
Memory, shared with a lover or
See passerby, moment for a
Selfie to capture a cool coast
Camped collection of breezes, which
The shutter will never expose

Laps lay parallel in a brief,
Exchange sharing tales of fortunes.
Lost and won to misbehavior,
A bed to countless mocked homeless,
A workplace as well, read the sign.
And offer a gratuity,
For the attended privilege.

Low perch for weary birds of prey.
An elevated lookout for
Pigeons, shrikes and the merry
mocking jay.

Rice Paper Plant

I can't grow among roses,
A lowly rice-paper plant
evergreen, and green as ever,
envious of their fickle foliage.
How they are adored in there
pinks, yellows, reds, and whites.

With no indifference to seasons,
my growth gives gourds of glib,
glamour to my lonely stalk.
I long for my blossoms to be
caressed by lovers turned to twilight.

My felty leaves lull to velvet petals,
that fume the bride's bouquet.
I reside in tranced torture of ever
flowering my globular umbels.
Deep down, doting a desire,
to be celebrated as a festive floret.

Scavenger's Waltz

Buzzard's reticent to a manic cry,
Circle overhead to a scavenger's waltz.

Bow and curtsy to windswept wing,
Passing ovals in ever-expanding orbits.

Waiting in tandem for the earliest decay,
A feinting carcass, spotted from the air.

Soaring to nature's aria in frenzied chorus,
Prancing talons hasten the inevitable fall.

Diving faster as death's aroma satiates the air,
The feast is at hand as the music refrains.

Cascading down with pious etiquette,
Devouring all that remains.

My Old Underwear

Nobody donates their old pajamas to the homeless,
nor underwear or socks. Practical holiday gifts have
no secondhand value. Blue jeans ok, overcoats, yes.
Save nothing that touches an undesirable or amorous
part of the human form.

What a peculiar life these garments lead once
christened
With DNA. Deemed unworthy, we pragmatize these
items
as too vulgar to display, killing the romantic mood.
Weathered,
they are familiar but unseen for their decay.

Spanish Moss

Like the old man's whiskers,
it bends and sways.

Playing silent chimes to nature's pious Psalm,
Torrid in appearance, while masking over
new life. Chainmail fungus.

A simple fervent cluster of moss,
tattered and frayed, will not cling to a hanged
man's grave.

Spare Me

My anthology of the dead has no pungent smell,
Cursing lines to avoid capture orate a living hell.

They tax my soul with wordy pikes percolating to the
river Styx,
Amused in rest bits of wasted guile far from utopia's
outer mix.

Give me shelter from this contrite rage; my escape has
not a clue,
Better I step forward, signaling my fast break on cue.

Slithering past a nightmare song, I jettison to a calmer
sea,
Gazing toward my journey, I arise from bended knee.

Superstition

The dog ate all my peanut butter,
The cat drank all my wine,
Kids drank milk from Holstein's udder.

Kiss your Ma and draw the shutter,
Treacherous omen, beware the sign,
The dog ate all my peanut butter.

Read tea leaves to Grandma's Putter,
Gather to the table, now we dine,
Kids drank milk from Holstein's udder.

Black cyclones will pitch away clutter,
Ropes to shelter, stay in line,
The dog ate all my peanut butter.

Babble tongue reveals morbid sputter,
Hug the walls, you'll be just fine,
Kids drank milk from Holstein's udder.

Deafening wind makes foundations stutter,
Ignore the howling betwixt and twine,
The dog ate all my peanut butter,
Kids drank milk from Holstein's udder.

Take a Ride to Selma

I sit on the back of the bus in reverence to,
former patrons who beheld their legal obligation.
Embrace to alleviate the medley of casual bias.

A heart full of shame for my ancestors, they found it,
vital to be indignant facing new.
Culture, New ideas, new markets, new relations,
pause in graffiti's gauntlet.

Placid coexistence is the prize we now take,
for granted. Seeds of social equity camouflage,
the jaundice seduced by appeasement.

Past my window I see a world of indifference for lack
of pigment.

The Duel

I challenge you to take up arms.
Your words ruffle my ego as a fly,
buzzing a wine goblet.

Dare I waste a shot on such
a futile transgression? Let us
trade pistols for spoons,

Penetrating the heart of a cold
blood pudding. Come,
sample buffet of compromised
conversation, toasting claims
to our absurd argument.

A sweet brag to past post-savored
glories will disarm
My son, one should not progress
from boyhood compromised to settle
a useless conflict. *Kill no man.*

Tour Guide

She introduced herself as Sarah,
like from the bible.
A frail little thing couldn't have
been more than nine or ten.
Gave me a wonderful tour of the
museum. Describing all the art and artifacts
in such esteem, one would think she
had been there a lifetime. Telling me
yarns about the heroic figures captured
in those old photographs, perplexing
to me, the conjugation of details in her
storied anthem, passing from room to room
like compartments in a time capsule.
I wandered into an adjacent room, then
suddenly, turning about, Sarah was gone.
Frantically, I captioned the curator for the
location of the lost little girl. The woman
assuaged my needless worry, then took me
to a private room where I was a gasp to see
a photograph of my charming guide
circa 1879. Sarah J Wilkes, born 1870,
died 1880 of smallpox. Apparently, others
receive Sarah's tour on occasion; she's very
selective about who is granted a special
chaperoned walk-through. Thank you, Sarah, my
posthumous lighting guide.

White Egret

One white egret in his gangly gawking gait,
reaches slightly above what
his awkward balance point will be tolerated.

Gracious in step, each digit meticulously placed
forward, finds equilibrium, passing
subtly, between footprints.

Raindrops, in their fluid fall, would not undo,
this fanciful walk tracing the garden's edge.

In constant motion, be it quite graced, would offer
safe passage to a quiet resting place.

A Song of Souls

Calico moons will pester your rippling.
gaze.
Souls of lacquered luster pitch and
bow in cool shadows.

Feast your eyes on what dotes beneath my heart.
Our song of souls will reverb fireflies, spurting
from the conductor's baton.

It teases a lover's heartstrings with red velvet melodies.
Fonts delight in salacious strain. Well, is the wisdom
being
undaunted by teasing vespers?

The beast within my heart has been conquered by your
velvet chord.

A Warrior's Fate

The principles of attrition in the minds of others
cannot stop the ongoing wars. The real enemies
are hidden in a breastplate reflection. A warrior's death
should occur without the sword and shield. No
campaign, no battle, just the glimmer of a single candle
glowing in the moonlight.

Kings wave to the parade as the Knights pass in review.
Ashamed of their roles as butchers of men, they weep
alone at the death of each troop who is to die loud
and angry, chocking on the irony of losing the one
thing
leaders of men hold so dear their bright golden army,
marching off to fight.

A cavalier fate awaits the good Knight when the sword
preys upon him as it has taken so many before. It is the
destiny of men to cherish evil deeds during battle. To
die a
hero's death is that separatist task that will secure a
legacy
in lore and song.

The battle is over now. The dead are piled like stacks of
kindling
ready for the hearth. The butcher among them with a
dagger in
his chest by his own hand. A martyred manumission
puts an

end   to   the   King's   tortured   soul.   Posthumous   decorations
draped over headstones pass valor to the survivors.

Acid Rain on My Pillow

Acid rain dampens my pillow again.
The door is left ajar initiating his walk
of shame. The same doorway that earlier
allowed passions to enter unscathed. Doting
and laughing together well into the night,
imposing insincere affection. It is destiny to
lay with insecure men.

Resting motionless in stoic silence, tears
saturate the pillow. They are cold, like
fading pastels quenched under morning dew.
The hope that once titillated my heartstrings
at happy hour is sufficiently squelched by
dawn. Forced to blot away the acid rain on
my pillow and start again.

Benny Bright, Keeper of the Christmas light

Benny Bright, keeper of the Christmas light,
adorns the tops of sacred trees on Christmas
eve night.

Little Benny Bright must be diligent in his plight
and illuminate every Christmas tree to guide
Santa in his flight.

Without Benny to light the way, Santa will
not fulfill his promise to all the children
before night turns to day.

If the tree lights go out, the kids will miss out.
Then, Sinister Brown, the Mayor of Youngster Town,
will get his wish and wear his gloomy, pointed crown.

Old Sinister has no love in his heart; after stealing
Benny's illumination chart. Now, his treasury will grow
as the children toil and sow.

Sinister will be feared by all and place every
child at his beck and call. Benny must create
a scheme to give the trees a brilliant gleam.

Santa's elves will help tonight to recover
the chart and make things right. With the chart
in hand, it will be the end of a sinister plan.

Bloody Boots

Blood from a bullet wound doesn't
cover the ground. It crawls over the dermis
with no conjecture as to its origin. Catch all
the congealed runoff as the surgeon plies
his trade.

Surface scars will heal before trepidations
release vested hands, as minor cuts confuse
coagulation of hearts pounding pasteurized
adrenalin.

Take my blood and underwrite a happy motif,
sweltering below a sundried scab. Pilfered
dominions stanch a worthwhile cause and tread
less toxic in bloody boots.

Garden for the Homeless

Watch the world through hazel eyes that reflect
an adhesive smile. I am ready to catch old leaves
that jolt around falling awry. The envy of winter
is swollen on my tongue.

Come inside and take a slice of hardship to the
garden. Rows of insignificance grow tall and
slender just beyond serenity. Hunger has
a bounty all its own, willowing in overbearing
irrigation.

The good straight-legged farmer dotes on his
harvest. Another year of raindrops filtered by
summertime, a tribute to the red clay delta, sipping
under the water tower.

Can a man find satisfaction in reaping less want? Still,
the water flows past poverty faster than deliverance.

Silent Swarey

Girls, I am quelled in the satisfaction of
silence. The hair, the lipstick, in bombastic
surrealist form, give me a stage and I will
play to your endorphin emotion. A glittered
adulation to dance, refrain in 6-inch heels.

Not a word is vocalized to a rightful, sustained
audience. Rant for the masses who maxim a
subliminal caucus to my vexations.

Devilish to erroneous playthings, we manicure
in harmonious social delights. Political frowns
are no match for sequin gowns.

Boisterous hues congregate in delightful macramé
schemes. A visual litigation in the absence of reverb.

Delegate a request to banish shelled statuesque
conformity. Phallic behaviors can't suppress the
quest for social balance. See the resemblance of me
intravenous and free.

Hardness

My love for you is anodized.
There in, not too soft, not deep either.

As newlyweds, we toiled in physical delights,
unlike old lovebirds who find passion
in dishpan hands

Daddy's love was never kind,
justified, all the same. Mommy's love was
penetrant, discarding slag from iron.

I love hard and fight for it,
drawing orchid nectar from cashmere abrasions,
passive attrition for the metal we make.

Lightning

When a trunk splits, two halves become more
than the whole. The rings have to choose sides.
Branches will collide in their advance toward
a gallant sky.

The leaves carry nevus of a dual personality. A
sibling debate with no conscience, just a natural
propensity to exfoliate under sun spots. Green to
yellow,
red to brown, so elegant to reverse shade at seasons
end, a tepid pill to swallow.

Bring harsh rain and wind to strip all foliage as
punishment for such septic work. Druids find no
shelter amid the grassy lea.

Lights Out

The day's luminescence is toggled to nightfall,
blankets cross a wet shoulder.
There is honesty in the un-kept neon.
Wind ebbs in the silence of late evening. Dew
will condense a chlorophyll fragrance to the
penetrating dawn.

Morning glows a host of imperfections. Shadows
on the artist's pallet run a gasp applied to the canvas.
My coffee is black until the advent of cream, savoring
the swirling aroma.

Love me in the absence of light. Gratitude will
exfoliate under darkness.

Looking Glass

One day, I went window shopping for
a broken piece of glass. The doorman
pointed through the panel to show clear, like resin.

His elbow separated the sill from the threshold,
unlike the window washer brandishing a
broken bottle. How to quell his thirst for jagged
Crystal shards in a pool of winter would never
put my curiosity to bed.

Both eyes focus at light speed and recognize the
uncut panel. Elusive, bouncing a bit from
inside the pillowcase. No edge so dull to penetrate
a thin, frustrating afternoon.

Sleep has to relate-
Mirror to mirror
Frame to frame
Pane to pane.

Mad in Blue

Turquoise surrounds the morning minutes before dawn. Heartbeats are rigorous following a delicious dream. The censoring of daylight is still the goal of waning eyelids, and morning breath is the motivation for the loo.

I am derelict to my pillowed partner, who dreams of cute cuddles washed away by a warm under-toe. All too actual, benign to the cavalier carnivorous conflict waiting on the front steps. Beyond the doorway, a moment of passive reticule as one passes by coffee houses and taxicabs.

Penance for a warm embrace, escargot, and chilled merlot pressed upon my nape, caressed by mad in blue.

Matriarch

At Mother's embrace, I bear no carnage
in the subtle sanctuary. Vows in randomness
can no longer bridge a doted caress. Please
it to a silent vesper passing over a childlike
gaze as moons speak of arid shadows.

Stand and wash a barely bridled breach to
castrate the wisdom of men like pastel foliage
unharvested in late seasons.

A barren chalice will ungulate fruitless in the
bane of motherhood. Zodiacs justify a speckled
brand left to promiscuity. An oratory bathed in
bronze will linger still.

My Kingdom Below the Mountain

My Kingdom is poor, unlike yours.
Sit next to me and count the grains
of sand that lay under my feet. Watch
the day pass tonight and hold back
your ration of pity.

My Kingdom is cold, unlike yours.
Ask me to sing you a lullaby so that I may
watch your happy dreams. Cover me in
stoic exhales that I may warm myself
against the night.

My kingdom is hungry, unlike yours.
Ask me to share my bread and wine
My emptiness is a penance to the
bounty of others.

My Kingdom is just, unlike yours.
Ask me for my life, it is all I have left
to give. Take my soul to your home
where cultural fondness rallies for
sympathetic alms.

Nectar

He watches over me as I dote among dandelions.
Fondling in captions of wildflowers, breathe in
nuance from each perfumed petal. A head above
stems amid bent hat pins, prolonged use in defense
of a dead bouquet.

A keen glance as workers bathe their queen in fresh
nectar. Sweet resin salivates while golden honey drips
onto my pointed tongue.

This conduit pleasure pleads sloth before consolidated
conscience. Turnabout to catch pollen particulates
with outstretched fingers, screening delicate wind
shear.

Passionate pastime for the beleaguered bumble bee.

Night Rain

Raindrops fall into blackness at night, despondent
to a precocious dawn. Black jewels flicker amid
platinum gaslights, they bounce and ricochet,
penetrating
Bermuda blades.

Droplets ping atop my forehead, chasing follicles,
mixing in
saline resin, destined to share space with groundswell.
Variable
darkness under a squinting moon sheds a festive
fragrance before a nasal fume.

Cupped hands will secure a quenched taste of clear
condensation,
set a mere tickling for the tongue as sheets saturate my
body in
shimmering ebony haze.

Reflection

My mirror tells many lies,
as images bode a sad reflection.
This basking frame surely belongs to another,
much younger self and shall morph,
this weathered vision before me.

Has my journey been so long,
a premonition of appearances yet to unfold.
Vanity would not tread so harsh on one's esteem
as to scorn such a character in middle age.
Once statuesque, bathed in musculature,
and hair flowing like water from Niagara.

Morning to night, my mirror tells little lies,
peeling away at previous prides.
I am not resolute to diminish my station, or
die in ignorance.
Volumes lay unwritten. My sage
ego is venom for unborn generations.

Ruthless

Open the umbrella and let others,
bid for your immediate grin.
Hurry to your hushed liaison with
fists clenched before a prism of passion.

Circumscribe the day into tiny candy thoughts,
raking sticks along pickets. Bathe in the sweetness
of honeycomb. Vanity will push away one's cowardice.
No guilt for the selfish, just another savory morsel.

Default to a reckless encounter and dine on words
which canker a lust for piety; I loathe the promiscuity
of your hapless tear. Share in the ordinary sloth that
spells my appetite, feeling your heart pulsate to
erstwhile
pleasure.

Spoken Flames

Pour water from a bottle, and the clock
runs backward down the staircase.
Droplets morph to vapor, penetrating former
dawns.

Evil deeds are not the will of bad tempers.
I, the bad man, touch the whorish flame and spit
burning
words to the wind. My eczema is a testament to inferior
salve.

Watch the fall and rise, a rolling canvas spilling day
from
night. Curses and salutations will pass over streams
smelling
of old aftershave. Power politics is narcotic and
penetrates
the skin like condensation drenching a weathervane.

Sweet Tooth

I eat all the fully formed candies
first, just to get to the sugared bits at the bottom of the
bag.
They are orphans.

Chopped, diced, and minced into a cold, isolated
corner
by concerted industrial confectionery cams and cogs,
only to be discarded by the more quality pieces.
The aristocrat's, crowding in the hermetically sealed
package,
stamped, labeled, and shipped to your favorite candy
aisle.

How arrogant they seem,
rolling and polishing each other to a
bright sheen by the journey's end.
That we share the same circumstances
pay them no matter what. Once the seal is broken,
they are eaten one by one,
waiting in anxious anticipation.
Pine for an avalanche to freedom.

Windswept Crossroads

Four sneezes will not make an epidemic,
watching horses gallop across a sea of
pollenated azaleas. Move along past the
concrete acreage while eagles make love at
eighty miles an hour.

Winds gather leaves in anticipation of winter,
smiling between breaths under an octagon frame.
Silly songs beat a spastic rhythm under massive
hoof prints.

The stallions march along floating ice bridges.
Oceans wave to the girl dressed in calico who
can't find a shallow patch of ground, hiding
from a blaze of scorched earth-covered granite.
Standing in a fog, waving farewell.